YOU
are a
BADASS®
EVERY DAY

ALSO BY JEN SINCERO

You Are a Badass at Making Money:
Master the Mindset of Wealth

You Are a Badass:
How to Stop Doubting Your Greatness
and Start Living an Awesome Life

The Straight Girl's Guide to Sleeping with Chicks

Don't Sleep with Your Drummer

YOU
are a
BADASS®
EVERY DAY

HOW TO KEEP YOUR MOTIVATION STRONG,
YOUR VIBE HIGH, AND YOUR QUEST FOR
TRANSFORMATION UNSTOPPABLE

JEN SINCERO

VIKING

VIKING

An imprint of
Penguin Random House LLC
penguinrandomhouse.com

Library of Congress Cataloging-in-Publication Data

Names: Sincero, Jen, 1965- author.
Title: You are a badass every day : how to keep your motivation strong, your vibe high, and your quest for transformation unstoppable / Jen Sincero.
Description: New York : Viking, [2018] |
Identifiers: LCCN 2018045770 (print) | LCCN 2018047810 (ebook) |
ISBN 9780525561651 (ebook) | ISBN 9780525561644 (hardcover)
Subjects: LCSH: Motivation (Psychology) | Success.
Classification: LCC BF503 (ebook) | LCC BF503 .S496 2018 (print) |
DDC 158.1—dc23
LC record available at https://lccn.loc.gov/2018045770

Printed in the United States of America
1   3   5   7   9   10   8   6   4   2

Set in Bembo MT Pro
Designed by Cassandra Garruzzo

To you, oh great and wondrous badass,
thank you for being who you are.

INTRODUCTION

I f you've ever read a book that felt like it was written just for you or listened to a talk that blew yer mind wide open or hung out with brilliant, big-thinking, butt-kickin' folk who made you feel like you could do anything, then you know how quickly you can get inspired to transform your reality, how effortlessly you can grasp the scope of your own mightiness, how easily you can become drunk with possibility. You also know you can slide down into inertia and doubt just as easily (okay, more easily). Sometimes mere hours (minutes?) after you walk out of the life-changing seminar, put down the book, kiss your butt-kickin' friends good-bye, the blinders of your present "reality" can start to block out the greatness you glimpsed for yourself. Before you know it, all your familiar excuses have shuffled back in and resumed their perches, planting their heavy, defiant bodies

1

squarely in the way of your hopes and dreams. Sometimes. But sometimes you make the hell-bent-for-glory decision to keep that meteoric momentum going strong and you do whatever it takes to change your life, making your old excuses feel suddenly awkward and embarrassed and desperate to find any reason to leave the room.

The excellent thing about living as a human being on planet Earth is that you have the almighty power of choice, which means you get to choose between achieving success and giving up. And the excellent thing about success is that it always comes down to one simple thing: the decision to keep going until you've reached your goal. Anyone can get excited about a great idea, but to stick with it all the way through to fruition is a whole other banana. Success requires commitment, motivation, focus, a sense of purpose, and courage, and it requires that you continually strengthen these muscles so you meet each new challenge with a big ole can of get-the-fuck-outta-my-way.

Strengthening these muscles of badassery is where something I like to call the *spiritual gym* comes in. As we travel the winding road to greatness, we've got to have some sort of workout routine to keep our motivation strong, our belief in the near impossible unwavering, and our focus firm—because muscles don't stay strong all by themselves. You don't go to the regular gym, for example, get in shape, and then act like, alrighty, that was great, thanks for the help with my awesome new bod, see ya! You have to keep working out on a regular basis, and you have to keep pushing yourself past your comfort zone if you want to stay strong.

Going to the spiritual gym involves any combination of the following:

- Studying self-help books, unearthing your limiting thoughts and beliefs, and doing the work to get over your blocks—even if the work includes stuff like cooing "You amaze me" into the mirror each morning or singing a love song to your shadow self. (You must be willing to do whatever it takes, no matter how excruciating.)
- Meditating.
- Listening to powerful speakers.
- Journaling.
- Making gratitude lists that leave you sobbingly aware of what a miracle your life is.
- Reading biographies of people who inspire the crap out of you.
- Exercising.

- Listening to music that makes you feel like an invincible pillar of joy, strength, and don't-mind-if-I-do.

- Saying affirmations over and over and over until they become your truth.

- Making a vision board and staring at it, all of the time.

- Ensmartening yourself.

- Breathing slowly, intentionally—deeply sucking in the good, fully breathing out the bad.

- Stretching.

- Writing down your manifesto and visualizing yourself in your new life to the point where you can feel it, taste it, own it, get all choked up and grateful for it.

Success isn't static, it's not one place, you don't arrive at success, crack open a beer, and call it a day. Success is a way of being and adapting and growing that gets easier the more you practice. If you want to be a successful person and stay a successful person, you're gonna want to always have some sort of spiritual gym workout in place. And you're going to want to be especially diligent about your workout when you're cranking away toward achieving a specific goal.

So . . . before you read the rest of this book, put together some kind of spiritual gym routine. Get specific about which practices make you feel like you could bench-press a gorilla and make them a nonnegotiable part of every single solitary day with no exceptions. Which song or playlist will you listen to every day? Which book or books will you read every morning and for how long? Will you meditate? For how long and where? You are unauthorized to wing it each day—get the specifics of your routine in place so you can commit to it without a bunch of fumbling around and indecision and trying to remember where you left your yoga pants. I recommend keeping your workout short so you don't get overwhelmed, ideally fifteen to thirty minutes per day, first thing in the morning.

This book is meant to be a supplement to your spiritual gym workout. It doesn't go deep into explaining how a lot of the concepts work, like my other Badass books and most self-help books do, but it gives you simple prompts to think about and put into action immediately. Think of it as the booster shot for all the motivational medicine you're taking. Or as your accountability partner, your personal trainer, your superhero pill, or as the keeper of the mighty flame roaring beneath your nether regions.

This book isn't meant to add to your workload but rather to make the work easier and more focused by giving you quick perspective shifts, reminders, meditations, and loving motivational spankings. Read a page a day or just open the book up at random when you need a boost and see what you get. I also suggest you use a journal with the book so you have a place to do the exercises and keep track of any insights you have while reading. If a particular exercise or affirmation is really working for you, keep doing it until you feel you need to move on to a new one and then consult a different page.

Here's to living the life you desire and deserve, every damn day!

t always surprises me when people say, "I'm not a very creative person." Because the thing is, if you're alive, you're creating. You're creating thoughts, friendships, new cells, hairdos, joys, problems, solutions, sentences, routes to work, truths to live by, perhaps the occasional avocado toast.

You are an artist and your masterpiece is your life.

- Your world is the canvas.
- Your desires and ideas are the sketches.
- Your thoughts, words, and attitudes are the paint.
- Your body is the brush.
- Your actions are the strokes.
- Your beliefs are the skills you use to apply the paint.
- Your faith and gratitude determine how extraordinary your work of art is.

If your painting isn't turning out the way you'd like it to, investigate which part of the process you're struggling to master and then change your approach. Are you taking bold, brilliant action but constantly whining about how hard everything is? Are you focused on your desires but lugging around deep-seated fears that you can't have what you want?

Each thought, feeling, and action is something you have the power to change. You are creating your reality. I repeat, *you are creating your reality*. How awesome is that?! Use your imagination, follow what feels right, play, push yourself, let it rip, and get good at making new, exciting choices that bring as much beauty into the world as possible.

onfidence is not something you need to acquire, it's already inside of you. It is you.

You were born with all the confidence and self-esteem in the world. In the beginning, you accepted yourself fully; thoughts of yourself stopped at "I am" and only later grew into, oh, say, "I am screwed because I can't do anything right." Any doubts or judgments or fears you have about yourself were learned over time—they are not the truth, they are just mental constructs. The truth is, you are perfect exactly as you are. You were made to be the you that is you, and there is no wrong way to be you because even if you try to be someone else, you're always being you.

Shut your beautiful eyes, breathe into your beautiful body, clear your beautiful mind, feel the life force that is you, revel in the spectacularly unique essence that is you and only you.

Out of all the billions of humans coming and going over time, there is, was, and will be only one you. That is worth appreciating. That is worth celebrating. That is worth loving.

If you run from your fears,
they will follow you.
If you run straight at your
fears, they will get the hell
out of your way. Fears hate it
when you do that.

. . . .

An excuse is simply a challenge that you've decided has power over you. If you're serious about changing your life, you'll find a way past all your obstacles; if you're kinda sorta serious about changing your life, you'll find an excuse. In other words, excuses are fake news.

We get extremely defensive about our excuses, because excuses free us from taking responsibility for our lives: "I didn't get fired because I have a bad attitude, I got fired because my boss is a chowderhead!" Excuses also help us avoid facing our fears and stop us from opening ourselves up to unknown possibilities that can only reveal themselves if we let our excuses go.

This is what we call staying in our comfort zone—staying in situations that range from the ho-hum to the full-on sucking simply because it's more "comfortable" than straying out into unknown territory.

Please do not waste your one and only chance to be the you that is you on planet Earth screwing around with excuses when you have the power to create whatever you desire.

I deserve and expect

good things.

. . . .

hatever we've got on repeat becomes our "reality"—what we look at every day, our thoughts, what we read, listen to, talk about, tell ourselves, etc.

This "repetition is reality" concept is the reason that repeating affirmations is so effective; why looking at your vision board over and over is so powerful; why hanging out with kick-ass people who talk about kick-assery is so important; why being diligent about being grateful is so transformative; why putting Post-it notes all over your house that say "I am special, I am loved, I am worthy" and then frantically running from room to room ripping them down when you realize your friends are at the door is so worth the risk.

Take stock of what you've got on auto-loop, and up-grade anything that's not supporting you in your quest for greatness. Pay attention to what comes out of your mouth when you talk to your coworkers, the thoughts that go through your mind when you look in the mirror or browse a dating site or watch TV. How do the books you read, the podcasts you listen to, the foods you eat, the newspapers you read, the people you hang with make you feel?

Write down five beliefs/complaints/activities/environments that are constant buzzkills in your life, and then write down the specific ways in which you will immediately upgrade them.

There's a lovely story about a woman who walks to a stream many miles away, fills her two clay pots with water, and carries them back to her house, dangling each pot from either side of a long stick that she drapes across her shoulders. When she arrives home each day with the water, one of the pots is full, and one is half empty. The half-empty pot is all sad and feels like a big fat loser because it's got a crack in it, and it beats itself up for wasting water, for doing a bad job, for not being as perfect or effective as the crack-free pot. It tells the woman how ashamed it is, but the woman thinks this pot is doing a fabulous job and tells it how the world is a better place because of its crack.

She explains that the path to the stream that she's walked every day for two years now has a stunning line of flowers growing along one side, thanks to the water that's dripped out of the pot. She tells the pot how much joy these flowers bring her every time she sees them and how they would never have been able to grow without the crack in the pot. She reminds the cracked pot that the side of the path with the flowers is full of life and color and bees and birds.

Everything in our "reality" is reflected back to us depending on how we choose to perceive it. Your "flaws" are either strikes against you or part of what make you unique and awesome—it's your choice. Find beauty in everything about yourself instead of beating yourself up or deciding you suck because you're not like everyone else.

Not only is loving yourself a more joyful way to walk through life, but you never know what brilliance might sprout up from your temporary failures. It's possible you will wind up creating something far more beautiful than what you set out to create, and that you would never have even known existed, if you hadn't "screwed up."

When it comes to the stuff that really matters to you, why settle for fine when fabulous is also on the menu?

· · · · · · · · · · · · · · · · ·

We need to be aware of what's happening in the news, and as human beings with beating hearts, it's often challenging to stay optimistic, high frequency, and useful in the face of all the scary/awful stuff going on in the world. So do pay attention, but don't smother yourself with so much depressing information you can no longer speak without sobbing. Figure out where your personal tipping point is, and when you feel yourself about to cross over from staying informed to becoming paralyzed by hopelessness, place your focus on something that lifts you up and energizes you. Transform your anger into action, channel your sadness into taking care of whomever you can however you can, use your shock to energize yourself to get involved with local activists groups. We're all here to make the world a better place, and we're no use to anyone, including ourselves, if we're immobilized by grief. Think about the massive positive change that could occur in the world if we each did even the tiniest thing to make a difference every single day.

The more you focus on the positive instead of getting sucked down by the negative, the more energy you'll have to help and the more light you'll bring to situations that sorely need it.

Breathing is one of the most centering, relaxing, and profound activities we've got going. By taking a few moments to stop, turn off your brain, and breathe deeply, you allow yourself the space and the focus to connect with Universal Energy and to tap into your most powerful self.

An excellent method for breathing deep down into your core is by imagining that you're "smelling the rose." When you smell a rose, you inhale all the way down to the bottom of your feet, you close your eyes, you're focused on the moment, you relish the breath, you fully expand.

Remember to stop and smell the rose as often as you can.

The Universe requests the honor of your presence at the raging cosmic bender through time, space, and infinite possibility otherwise known as your one and only life.

What are you bringing to the party: your drab old pile of sob stories or your dancing shoes?

Remember that the little tasks you've set up for yourself have importance above and beyond simply the doing of those tasks in the moment. Your "reality" is made up of all the bits and pieces of your everyday life, like a pixelated picture made up of trillions of tiny dots. No matter how small a task is, when it's in the direction of your goal, it adds to your progress, so you're gonna want to treat it like the big deal it is. If you're studying French, for example, and you've made the decision to learn two new words a day, do it. Think about how many words that will add up to in a couple of months!

The next time you're feeling lazy or like you've got too much going on to do X, remember that all the tiny bits matter in a very large way. Here's an affirmation you can use to keep your eye on the ball: "This moment is a vital part of a whole life that I'm creating. What I choose to do in this moment defines who I am and how I show up in the world. I'm dedicated to creating an extremely awesome life for myself, so I'm taking this moment seriously, getting the hell on it, and staying in excited expectation of the stupendousness hurtling toward me."

You are beautiful.

. . . .

Even though we often choose to give them immense power over us, cravings, distractions, and really bad but kinda fun ideas are all, in reality, extremely fleeting and wimpy blips that quickly pass through our consciousness.

The trick to resisting these temptations and staying the course to success is to focus on the fact that not only are our negative impulses wimpy and fleeting, but so is the immediate gratification they so seductively dangle before us. For example, next time you're tempted to smoke a cigarette, keep in mind that not only will the craving only last a couple of moments, but so will the satisfaction you get from smoking that cigarette. Train your focus on something else for a handful of seconds, like the image of your pink, healthy lungs giving you a standing ovation, and before you know it the craving will pass. Or next time you sit down to work and get distracted by the thought that you haven't checked your mail today, remember that this thought can leave your mind as quickly as it popped in, and that seeing what's in the mail will be far less satisfying than getting your work done. Or next time you're getting ready to go to Pilates and realize that happy hour starts in a couple minutes, remember that you can move this thought out as quickly as you allowed it in and that the long-term effects of working out far outweigh the immediate, and naughty, thrill of day drinking.

Not-so-great thoughts, impulses, and ideas only grow if we feed them. If you're pretending you're addicted to the sugary pull of immediate gratification brought on by negative impulses, keep in mind that staying disciplined is simply a matter of waiting and refocusing, it's not some untamable beast.

Living a life in which you're constantly letting yourself down and feeling powerless against distractions and impulses is hard; waiting a few seconds and retraining your focus to achieve success is easy.

Find yourself a mastermind partner or a mentor or a coach or someone you have to answer to on a weekly or biweekly basis. We are so much more likely to stretch ourselves, or even just show up, if someone else is involved. It's why people get running partners and personal trainers and join study groups—we could pursue our goals on our own, but because we don't want to look like a boob in front of others, and because two minds are more powerful than one, we get better results when we team up with awesome people.

You have countless things all around you at every moment to be in awe of, grateful for, excitedly tugging on people's sleeves about, squeeing in delight over, motivated by, in love with. All you have to do is remember to pay attention.

Contrary to popular belief, it's not as important to know exactly what you want to do with your life as it is to know what makes you feel good. We tend to put more importance on logical thinking, on making lists, on having a plan that's all mapped out and reasonable and shipshape. While all of that is good, we sometimes plan our lives without making a priority of letting ourselves be, do, and have the things that bring us joy. Our brains have been in the spotlight for so long, we've lost touch with—and learned to mistrust—this other, more intuitive side of ourselves.

Practice paying close attention to how different people, thoughts, places, ideas, things, the vision of your achieved goals, songs, activities, foods, clothing make you feel and let the good feelings guide you through your day. Imagine that your brain was removed from your body and all you had to use to make your everyday decisions were your feelings. No logical thinking. No memories of how things are or how they'll probably turn out, no judgments or fears that you'll look like an idiot, disappoint someone, or break something and have to gently prop it back up and hope no one notices or guesses it was you who broke it. How would that change things for you? Try moving through an entire day really noticing and responding to how things feel in your gut with as empty a mind as possible and write down anything you notice that's different.

DISCLAIMER: Yes, we must all do things we're not totally in love with like wait on hold with the IRS for forty-five minutes or get knee-replacement surgery, but I'm talking about strengthening the muscle that connects you to your inner compass so you can incorporate as much good-feeling-led decision making into your life as possible.

I'm. Fucking. Doing. This.

. . . .

D rink twice as much water as you usually do today. Hydrating is one of those things that's so simple and beneficial and important and yes, I know, annoying, because you have to pee all the time. But this is your one and only body we're talking about here. Considering the fact that the majority of your body is made up of water; and considering the fact that the better care you take of your body, the more energy you have; and considering the fact that it takes a whole lot of energy to transform your life, drinking a buttload of water seems like a pretty reasonable request to me.

Set a timer today and every hour get up and drink a large glass of water. If you can get into the habit of hydrating, the benefits far outweigh the weensy inconveniences.

When you feel frustrated or upset by a person or a situation, remember that your reactions are not the truth about the person or situation, they are just your feelings about them. All you have to do is change your perception and you are free.

used to hang out with this guy who was obsessed with thoughts that giant pieces of space debris could slam into the Earth at any minute and scatter our parts like dandelion seeds. He was also totally grossed out by restaurants—"You don't know whose eyebrows may have shed in your food." One time, I picked him up at the airport and watched him white-knuckle it all the way home. "How can you blindly trust all these other drivers?" he whispered. "You have no idea what they're going to *do*!"

Although we referred to him as the Phobe and some-times entertained ourselves by taking a sip out of his soda so we could watch him pretend not to want anymore, he did have a point. There are countless things to freak out about in this world—just getting out of bed in the morn-ing is somewhat arrogant in the face of it all. But there are also infinite things to be in a really good mood about, and since your reality is shaped by what you choose to focus on, if you want to live an enjoyable life, be diligent about what you pay attention to.

I bring up my friend and his obsessions because we are all, to some degree, the Phobe. We've all got our fears and limiting beliefs that we cling to and that can seem very real and big to us (I know, for a fact, he was putting on a bit of an act), but that probably seem blown out of proportion to the people around us. Think about it: when you see your wonderful, adorable friend worried about leaving his unappreciative, fun-free girlfriend because he's scared he'll be alone forever, you're not terribly concerned for him.

Clinging to fear, doubt, and worry doesn't protect you from the things you're fearing, doubting, and worrying about anyway—but it does make you experience your worst-case scenario before it happens, if it even happens at all (which, let's be honest, is not usually the case with our fears, doubts, and worries). It's like hitting yourself in the head with a rock all day so you can be prepared in case something falls out of the sky and hits you in the head.

Enjoy the present moment instead of wasting it by trying to predict future unsavory events that may or may not happen. Focus on stuff that energizes you and propels you forward, not on stuff that makes you paranoid and terrified and covered in an alarming amount of hand sanitizer. If we do get hit by a giant piece of space debris or if your business does tank or if you do get your heart broken, so be it. All worrying will do is make you live through the misery twice.

S pend a couple of minutes in silence with your eyes closed and visualize yourself standing in the new life you're presently focused on manifesting. Notice the details of your environment, feel your feelings, watch how you carry yourself, notice how you dress, what you think about, what you do.

Now open your eyes and go about your day today as if you're still in that environment, as if you've already reached success, as if you're presently the person you're becoming. Cop the knowing, happy attitude of the future you who's already achieved this super-exciting thing.

Acting as if your new life is already here is one of the most powerful things you can do, because when you match your energy to that of the new reality, you open yourself up to finding the path to get there.

There is no riskier risk than

refusing to risk at all.

. . . .

Take your favorite complaint, turn it inside out, and make it your new favorite affirmation.

For example: "I can't afford it" becomes "Money loves me so much it throws itself at me."

"I'm exhausted" becomes "I'm excited to meet my day and this excitement gives me energy."

"I hate my job" becomes "I'm grateful to my job for supporting me and for being a stepping-stone on my way to awesomeness and for teaching me so very very much about patience."

Write down whatever affirmation you come up with, tape it to walls all over your house, stick it to the dashboard of your car, needlepoint it onto a throw pillow and say it every time your catch yourself about to launch into your soon-to-be ex-favorite complaint.

When you commit to transforming your life, you commit to getting very uncomfortable over and over and over again.

Befriend the unfamiliar, the risky, the me no wanna. The discomfort means you're almost there.

Start seeing your low points and temporary failures as starting points. Instead of giving the many mishaps in your life the power to destroy you with disappointment, instead of hightailing it out of there by any means possible (including unsustainable, unhealthy, self-destructive means), instead of labeling yourself a giant loser who will never get it right, hang around for a minute and appreciate the architecture of your fail— learn from it; be curious about it; and if it applies, be impressed by just how colossally gigantic a fail it was! And then carefully, thoughtfully, and with a robust sense of humor, plot a new and better way up and out. You're so lucky to have a clean slate to start from, with nothing to lose.

When you stand up for yourself, you give everyone the opportunity to grow taller too.

· · · · · · · · · · · · · · · · ·

Before you sit down each day to work on transforming your life, spend a few moments ridding yourself of distractions. Turn off your phone, disable the internet, remove books or magazines from your workspace that don't apply to the task at hand, pile furniture in front of your door to keep your kids out . . .

Getting clear on what throws you off track and removing those interruptions temporarily from your life is such a simple and hugely helpful gift you can give to yourself, especially nowadays when we're so inundated with technological distractions it's like trying to get work done in the middle of a water balloon fight.

Take a few moments to set yourself up for success and you'll get there a hell of a lot faster.

The Universe has my back.
Everything I need to manifest
my desires is lining up for me
right now.

. . . .

D o something today that you've been talking about doing forever.

Buy a new mattress and get rid of that lumpy old one, sign up for tango classes, call your friend who you never see and invite him over, clean out the shed, book a trip to South Africa, quit smoking, file for a divorce, embrace your foot fetish, get a puppy.

The sooner you change your life for the better, the longer you get to live with those awesome changes. Stop screwing around and just do it already.

An "aha moment" is great, but an "aha permanent new way of life" is much better. Next time you have a mind-blowing flash of insight, write it down, then dig deeper to pinpoint the details of what shifted for you; record how the shift makes you feel and all the details of how you now think, believe, and approach life differently. (This will take all of five minutes and could really, oh, you know, transform your entire reality—so don't skip it!)

Read and viscerally absorb these details of your aha moment every day after it happens. I also recommend coming up with an aha mantra where you basically repeat your aha moment over and over so it becomes part of you.

If you really want the humdinger that just blew in and made all your hair stand up to stick around, you have to spend some time massaging it into your being or else it will fly out of you as quickly as it flew in.

S it in a quiet place, in a comfortable position. Imagine your brain is a tightly closed fist as you tense all the muscles in your face, your neck, your shoulders, your stomach, your butt, everything. Hold it all tight for five seconds and then release, imagining the fist that is your brain loosening, relaxing, and sending calming energy down through your head to every part of your body and out your fingertips. Focus on your breath moving in and out of your lungs, notice the weight of your body connecting with our dear old Earth, feel the energy tingling through you and imagine it connecting to all that is in the Universe—the drizzling rain, the planets, the brilliant ideas, the people, the hopes, the dreams, the dogs, the horses, the excitement, the tangerines, the plants, the laughs, the tears, the endless sea of love that flows through all of us and is all of us.

You are Universal Energy, you are love, you are a badass.

Herein lies the definition of stress: when you make the unhelpful choice to lose your sense of humor, your ability to shift your perspective, and your belief in your own superhero powers to deal with a challenging situation that you probably won't even remember in the not-so-distant future.

There are no stressful situations—only stressful ways of perceiving situations. And lucky for you, you are in control of your thoughts. The next time a challenging situation presents itself, take a pause and make the conscious choice to meet it with curiosity or humor or the knowledge that this too shall pass. You have nothing to gain by freaking out.

make the conscious effort to eliminate the following low-vibe phrases from your vocabulary today:

I want

I should

I wish

I can't

I'm trying

I don't know

Make the conscious effort to fill your vocabulary with the following high-vibe phrases today:

I choose

I can

I enjoy

I create

I love

I rock

The answers are on their way.

What comes out of your mouth comes into your life, so choose your words wisely.

When you remember that you're riding on a ball in infinite space with a humongous star of molten fire exploding over your head and that simply being alive is a near-death experience, the concept of playing it safe suddenly seems as ridiculous as it is. Heed the hollerings of your heart, grab hold the horns of uncertainty, and steer the snorting beast in the direction of your wildest dreams.

When you succumb to fear,
you are under the illusion
that you can predict the
future.

. . . .

I am so delighted and grateful to be _____.

Fill in the blank with your favorite scenario (a multi-millionaire, in a loving and committed relationship, my ideal weight of 145 pounds, healthy as an ox, the proud mom to two great kids, clear about my next steps, banjo-pickin' champion of the world, etc.). Say it all day long. Feel it. Believe it. Own it. Be it.

A simple, yet profound, habit that will help you stay the course and just generally live a more jolly life is the practice of setting intentions.

Intentions allow you to go about your day with clear goals instead of taking everything as it comes. Intentions also train your brain to stay conscious and present in the moment instead of stumbling around on autopilot while your unconscious, knee-jerk reactions run amok.

Here are some examples of daily intentions:

- I intend to take nothing personally today, especially nothing that my ex-husband says.
- I intend to say only lovely things about people today, myself included.
- I intend to get three new clients today.
- I intend to eat only healthy foods today.

- I intend to enjoy paying my bills today.
- I intend to sit up straight all day today.
- I intend to do something that scares the crap out of me and will push me toward my financial goal today.

I love this exercise because it helps you focus on just one day at a time, which is the key to fending off overwhelm and staying committed. You can do anything for one day.

You can also set an intention before a specific moment in order to stay woke and to employ your mighty power of conscious choice.

For example:

- Before walking into a room full of people: *I intend to be relaxed and present and look at my cell phone precisely zero times.*
- Before driving to the supermarket: *I intend to be blown away by the miracle that is driving a car followed by the miracle of all that food at my fingertips.*
- Before working out: *I intend to be present in my body and stay grateful for all it does for me.*

- Before visiting a grouchy relative: *I intend to have compassion for my uncle whose hip never stops hurting.*

- Before taking a bite of a grilled cheese sammich: *I intend to savor this bite and taste every nuance of its cheesy magnificence until I burst into tears of delight.*

Intentions are extremely powerful and blessedly simple because they break things down into bite-size tasks, keep us focused, enable us to show up as our best selves, and, you know, make things kinda fun.

Over the course of the average human being's lifetime, an alarming amount of time and energy is focused on thinking about how stupid/inconsiderate/evil/wrong other people are and coming up with the ways in which we are so much righter and smarter, and then getting on the phone to tell our friends about how stupid/inconsiderate/evil/wrong people are and how much righter and smarter we are. It's so . . . do I even need to say it?

Time is a finite commodity. You are on a mission, you understand how precious each little drop of time is, and you ain't got any to spare on low-vibe little craptastic endeavors like bitching and moaning. If someone is working your last nerve to the point where you're having trouble getting them off your mind (even after you've confronted them), use the fact that they're stuck in your mind to deepen your spiritual practice. View their behavior with the understanding that we are all human, we all have struggles, we all feel pain, and we all express ourselves in unique ways. Remember that you often have no idea what other people are going through. Maybe someone is acting like a belligerent asshat because their spouse just asked them for a divorce and they're brokenhearted or they're driving like a maniac because they're rushing their kid to the hospital or they're being flaky and unresponsive because they just discovered they have a lump. Giving people the benefit of the doubt is excellent practice for not taking stuff personally, and it gives you room to focus on more beneficial aspects of your life than on how pissed off you are. If none of this works and you're still having trouble shaking your irritation, picture the offending party wearing a pancake as a hat.

You do not have to love everyone or even like everyone, but badasses do have to rise above, grasshopper. Finding compassion is one of the most effective ways to earn your flowy spiritual robes.

The moments between waking and sleeping are such powerful times to connect to your intuition, your pal the Universe, and the calm knowingness of your limitless power that's trying to reach you through the buffalo stampede of everyday life.

When you first wake up, please, oh, please don't get sucked into your phone or computer or your to-do list. Stay in that juicy space of in-betweenness, be still for even just ten minutes, and bask in the awareness that you are a multidimensional, spiritual creature capable of transcending the limitations of your conscious mind.

Write down five accomplishments you're proud of, five things you love about yourself, five things you love about your body, and five things you love about the life you've created so far.

Read your list over and over all day. Write down any beliefs that shift for you or any aha moments that come up.

How determined you are
determines how successful
you are.

. . . .

Find someone who has succeeded at what you aim to do and figure out how they did it. Research their background, hire them as a consultant, take them out for a Reuben and pick their brain. There's no need to reinvent the wheel, and those who've gone before you can save you an insane amount of time, money, and heartache by sharing what they've learned. Plus, surrounding yourself with proof of what's possible is the best way to sustain an excellent, I'ma make this happen for myself, attitude.

More than any of our other senses, our sense of smell can completely captivate and surround us in its singular world. Smells can instantly call up emotions, calm us down, provide clarity and focus, motivate us, heal us, balance us, and make us time travel: "This shoe store smells exactly like my elementary school cafeteria!"

Spend some special time with your nose today. Stop along the street and smell the roses. Literally. As well as any other fragrant flower or gust of air or perfumed lady you happen to pass. Buy a lavender pouch or some essential oils or bring some flowers inside and put them in a vase. Relish the incredible, and often totally overlooked, world of scents and follow your nose to feeling happy and grateful.

know that one of my big challenges here on Earth is learning to master (or even acquire a tiny smidge of) patience. Because the Universe always gives us exactly what we need, I currently find myself living in a historical town full of elderly seniors who refuse to surrender their driver's licenses, lost tourists, fifteen-mile-an-hour speed limits, and endless mazes of narrow, confusing streets.

The other day I got trapped behind someone who was so lost/incompetent/dedicated to helping me grow that I was forced to sit through not one, but two rounds of light changes, ladies and gentlemen, while they tried, and failed, to make a left turn. I heard myself yelling, "Oh my God, I hate you!" only to immediately afterward mumble, "Here I go, it's happening right now."

In order to change unwanted behavior patterns, it's helpful to become aware of what sets us off so we can practice catching ourselves in the act. The moment you realize the not-so-great behavior is rearing its head, you can interrupt it by saying something like, "Here I go, it's happening right now." Then step back to watch yourself and make a more impressive choice about how to respond. As I sat there at the intersection, embarking on round three of Will This Person Finally Make the Turn?, instead of fantasizing about following them around for the rest of the day while leaning on my horn and screaming obscenities out the window, I sat back, rolled down my window, and looked at the flowers growing in the median. The exciting and educational conclusion to this story is that I made it to my doctor appointment with two whole minutes to spare.

Take a moment to think about which situations/people tend to trigger your not-so-favorite sides of yourself: Who or what inspires you to turn into a grouch, get gossipy, apologize unnecessarily, cheat on your diet, whine and complain, make excuses, talk badly about yourself and/or others, throw temper tantrums, overdo it with the tequila shots? Once you wake up to your danger zones, you're better prepared to catch and shift your behavior before you do something you regret.

Treat yourself to something special today.

. . . .

True power comes from thinking what you want to think, regardless of how things appear or what other people say or how impossible your ideas may seem. Your thoughts are what lead the charge through all the obstacles, doubts, and dark nights of the soul that are standing between where you find yourself now and where you're headed.

Think courageously, think largely, think audaciously, think magically.

It's impossible to hold on to
the past and seize the day at
the same time.

. . . .

C hoosing to hang with people who light you up and lift you up is a requirement for badassery. Refusing to share your finite and precious time on Earth with toxic, cranky-ass energy suckers who don't bring anything to the party (except perhaps a bucket of turds) is also a requirement for badassery.

If there's anyone in your life who's a negative force, make the decision right now to deny them access to you. Or as little access as possible, if they sit next to you at work or live with you. Do not share your hopes and dreams with them. Be busy every time they want to hang out. Take forever to respond to their texts and emails and eventually stop responding at all. Phase them out of your life. If they don't take the hint, you're going to have to explain that you've moved on. Breaking up is never fun, but the good news is the conversation usually goes real quick. Two minutes of pain for a lifetime of freedom. And I know it's never fun to hurt someone's feelings, no matter what the circumstances, but it's important to look at the breakup with someone toxic as you being nice to yourself, not as you being mean to them.

Putting on your grown-up pants and giving the heave-ho to toxic people not only beats the hell out of dragging around the dread of dealing with them, but if you're unhappy in the relationship, you'll be doing them a favor as well by letting them go.

Stand up. Stretch up your arms. Grab your wrist and stretch to one side and then do the same for the other side. Bend over and reach for your toes. Slowly roll up to standing. Drop your hands to your sides. Close your eyes. Breathe. Deeply. Five times. Think about how lovable you are and how much you love the people you love. Repeat all day.

all someone and tell them you love them. Call, as in pick up the phone, not as in send a text. You don't need to make a big deal of it; just call and tell them you were thinking about them and about how much you love them and you just wanted to let them know. The end.

You are a magical creature who lives in a magical Universe. Stay with me here. I know it sounds like we're going down Unicorn Lane but this is really important. When you step back from your everyday earthly life and remember that you are a spiritual being who is one with the energy of an infinite Universe, you suddenly won't have the patience for things like worrying that you'll never get into medical school or that your butt is too big or that someday that picture of you doing a beer bong in a tube top will end up on the internet.

Trust in the Force, grasshopper. If you can think it, and you desire it, and you align your thoughts, words, and actions with it, you can manifest it. There is no need to play small, to shrink back from anything that you fear is too big, too impossible, too out there. You are a boundless being; open wide your mind to possibility and leap largely into your life.

ake eye contact with, and notice the eye color of, as many of your fellow humans as possible today. Also, smile at them. And if you're feeling especially daring, engage them in conversation. Notice any feelings or observations that come up. Write down anything you've learned from this experience that you want to make a regular part of your everyday, happier, more connected life.

Success = your dreams + fear

+ doing it anyway

. . . .

have a friend who spent the majority of her adult life single. For years she tried, and failed, to find the man of her dreams. She went on 4,910 online dates, sat through countless awkward setups orchestrated by well-meaning friends and family, meditated, wrote in her journal, made vision boards, got her legs waxed, flirted, joined clubs, sometimes succeeded and sometimes failed to believe true love would ever find her. Eventually she met a guy at a party that some of her friends were throwing, and now she's happily married with a great kid and she can barely even remember what her past, lonely-hearted life felt like.

When we reach our goals, eventually they become our new normal. We settle into our new lives and forget how magnificent an accomplishment it is that we're where we are now.

Take a moment and think about all the things that once seemed so impossible/far away/never gonna happen for you and about which you're now like, "Oh, this old thing?" Maybe you felt like you were never going to lose the weight and now your trimmed-down bod is just your normal body. Or maybe you were always scrounging for cash and obsessed with how you were going to afford to take the bus to work and now money flows to you easily and you rarely think about it anymore.

Take stock of the new normals in your life. Really take the time to dig deep. Then write them all down and stare at them like the miracles they are. If you can do all that, you can do anything.

ake the conscious effort to stay present and do your best with every single endeavor you undertake today. If you're washing the dishes, notice the sound of the water, feel the squish of the sponge, and pay close attention to getting every little bit clean. If you're listening to your friend describe the seemingly endless dream she had last night, really listen to her, be fully present and available, connect with what she's going through, marvel at the staggering creativity of her subconscious mind, be the best friend she's ever had. If you're working out at the gym, connect with your body, be aware of the miracle that is being able to bend your knee, push yourself past where you usually stop.

Make this your most purposeful day on Earth, win the Gold Medal for Excellence in every category from communicating with your partner to building your business to being the best damn letter mailer ever to enter the post office.

Write down any specific actions or thoughts that made a huge difference in your results today and make a point to repeat these thoughts and actions until they become habits.

ome up with an image that represents your personal sanctuary. Maybe it's sitting along a stream in a beautiful forest or lying in an open field of flowers watching the clouds slowly pass overhead or cuddling in the arms of your soul mate while staring over the desert at a full moon or sitting on a cold metal bench eating a corn dog at a mud wrestling match in Queens. Find a comfortable, quiet place to sit, close your eyes, and call up the image of your sanctuary in your mind. Stay focused on the image, feel the air of your imagined world on your skin, hear the sounds, be there fully. Whenever thoughts try to barge their way in, place your focus back on this silent image and connect with all the feelings and energy of being there. Do this meditation as often as possible, and for at least ten minutes at a time.

Waiting until you know exactly what you're doing or until all of the circumstances are just right or until you have a large pile of extra cash lying around is the best way to wake up at ninety-seven years old, fishing your teeth out of a cup by the bed, wondering what the hell happened to the life you were so excited to live. Procrastination is just fear in the form of brakes, and fear is not the boss of you.

Start. Right. Now.

And here's a tip: start small. Chunk your to-dos down into manageable bits of time or break your tasks up into friendly little baby steps instead of trying to get the entire thing done in one intimidating leap. Especially if what's been dogging you is something you've been successfully putting off for a while. For example, if you're struggling to commit to a meditation practice, sit in silence for seven little minutes a day, then after a while up it to eight minutes and then nine and then you're on your way. If you're writing a book, sit at your desk with your phone turned off, the internet disabled, armed guards at your door, and do not get up until you've written one brilliant paragraph. The next time you show up for work write two brilliant paragraphs, then up it to three, and then four, and then you're on your way.

Motivation, commitment, focus—these are all muscles that, like any muscle, require strengthening. If you push yourself too hard right out of the gate, you'll hurt yourself and walk in wide circles around that gym instead of going inside whenever you're in the neighborhood. If you build slowly and steadily and chunk it down, not only do you save yourself some pain, but you'll start noticing changes almost immediately. And there ain't nothing that makes you show up, and keep showing up, like getting results.

I release regret, shame, and guilt. I embrace the absurd magnificence of the cosmic joke called life.

. . . .

f you're not getting the results you desire, figure out what you can do differently instead of pushing harder.

Can you shift your focus from one task to another? I know someone whose business was stalled after years of steady growth. He was working his rear end off, but nothing changed until he realized that because his business was cranking, he had so much more on his plate that he no longer had the space to focus on sales, which he loved and was great at. So he delegated almost everything that didn't have to do with sales, got back to selling, and his business started kicking butt again.

Can you come at your roadblock from a completely different direction, perhaps even act as if you're someone else? For example, if you're out there in the dating world and have gone out with a stream of duds, try dating someone who's not your "type."

Can you change your attitude? Dig deep and see if you can excavate any hidden doubt, fear, worry, crankiness due to impatience, etc. Then turn that frown upside down.

Can you take bigger risks? Can you reach out and ask someone to help you see something you might be missing? Can you do something so unexpected you surprise even yourself?

Get in your car, drive somewhere isolated, roll up the windows, and scream your head off. Set a timer and do this for three whole minutes, as loudly and forcefully as you can, without stopping and with the fervor and dedication of a person on fire. Literally and figuratively.

If you don't have a car, find The Biggest and Most Stifling Pillow in the World and scream into that.

When you're done, sit back, breathe, relax, and notice how freaking awesome that felt. Repeat as often as you can.

You have every single thing you need within yourself to make manifest whatever you desire. The desire itself came from the same place that the physical manifestation of this desire comes from. They are one and the same; they cannot exist without each other because they *are* each other. Trust in the truth that thoughts and things are the same stuff. Believe it (I mean, why the hell not? What do you have to lose?). Rejoice in it, get all stuck up about it, and go about your life with the knowledge that all you desire is right here, right now. The opportunities, the brilliant ideas, the new car, the person you want to meet, the money, they already exist in the Universal consciousness and they're already on their way to you in the physical plane. Your job is to shift any negative beliefs that are holding you back; align your thoughts and energy with that of your new "reality" and take decisive, fearless action so the physical manifestation of your desires can come running into your lovin' arms. In other words, you have to get out of your own way.

This affirmation will help you step aside and receive:

I am whole, I am complete, everything I desire is already here.

Every time you come from a place of "I need to get X" today, flip that impulse around and make it about giving.

For example, if you realize you're out of toothpaste, instead of focusing on getting some, focus on giving the drugstore your business; on giving the employees a smile and a hearty "Thank ye mucho!"; on giving thanks that you have the money, bodily ability, and transportation to make this dental adventure happen; on giving your teeth the love and attention they deserve, etc.

Do this all day with everything and take note of how that flip shifts your energy, your focus, and your results.

You are doing a great job.

. . . .

Have you ever noticed how when you vacation somewhere new, you're so much more open, you engage with more people, notice so many more things, feel more alive, expect the unexpected, explore more, enjoy more, eat stuff you never thought you'd put anywhere near your open mouth?

When we're on an adventure in a new surrounding, it's like time and space take on completely different, more vibrant qualities than they do when we're doop-de-do-ing through our routine, everyday lives. It's like you're wearing a special travel perfume that attracts a different reality to you.

Decide that today you will spray on the travel perfume and be a stranger in your own land. Treat everything in your world like it's brand-new—get out of your rut, take a different route to work, wear a hat if you never wear one, speak to strangers if you normally keep to yourself, shop at a different supermarket, eat at a new restaurant, sleep on the other side of your bed, shower in the guest-room shower, road trip to somewhere new, wear a fanny pack and a visor and ask people for directions.

Mix it up today and notice any brilliant observations that come up or any wonderful surprises that you'd like to incorporate into your everyday life.

lose your eyes and conjure up an image of yourself living in your ideal reality. Get as many specifics in place as possible and when you feel the wave of joy and excitement rush through you, notice where in your body you feel it. Is it in your chest? Your gut? Your head? If no feeling hits you right away, stay in that space of visualizing your most joyful world and keep sinking deeper and deeper into the details of it until you get a visceral reaction.

Once you've identified where in your body you feel the tingling of excited anticipation, make a point to keep placing your hands there all day today and conjuring up that feeling.

The more grounded you become in the energy of your new reality, the sooner that new reality will take form in the physical world.

Put a moratorium on complaining today. Every time you catch yourself about to launch into a disgruntlement, pause, breathe, and look for the lesson in the situation instead, or find something to be grateful for in what you're currently perceiving as nastiness. Be diligent about this all day long and notice how easy or difficult it is to shift gears, notice if doing so changes your energy, notice if editing your complaints makes it hard to talk, notice if it opens you up to different experiences, notice if you think it would be awesome to repeat this exercise tomorrow too.

Our realities are
make-believe—whatever
we make ourselves believe,
we experience.

. . . .

When I lived in Barcelona in my twenties, with my friend Jason, we rented a couple of rooms in a big apartment full of strangers (strange ones, believe you me). The building was in an old part of the city that used to be fancy, but that had deteriorated into rows of crumbling, ornate tenements. Our place was marked by giant, bombed-out-looking holes in its façade, junkies sleeping in its sweeping stairwells, and graffiti scrawled in Spanish across its massive entryway doors encouraging readers to "suck my balls."

Jason and I rented adjoining rooms, each of which came with high ceilings, windows to match, a tiny balcony overlooking the street, and a creaky and questionably habitable single bed. We had little money and even less stuff, so every Monday night we'd go "shopping" in the streets, picking through the treasures our neighbors put out for garbage collection the next morning. I don't know if it's because my twenties have taken on the fairy-dusted sparkle of youthful times long past or if Barcelona really was a magical city back then or if the hash we were smoking was as good as we bragged it was, but everything we desired seemed to be hidden beneath a ham shank in the trash. "Look, a Walkman! And it still works!"

One of my most lasting and cherished memories is of Jason flinging open the heavy French doors that connected our rooms every morning and floating in wearing this glitzy brocade robe he had found in the garbage. He'd carry in a mirrored tray (also garbage), sit on the end of my bed (which should have been in the garbage), hand me a chipped glass of cheap champagne, and ask, "What shall we celebrate today?"

We'd then sip and celebrate that it was a beautiful morning or that we got to live in Spain or that the prostitute down the hall had clearly moved from her home office to one out of earshot, or the fact that it was Monday—shopping! Or that Paolo, who didn't know I was alive yet, would soon fall madly in love with me.

Now that I'm older and wiser, I understand that these were not just the tipsy ramblings of happy-go-lucky youths, but the kind of gratitudinal thinking that leads to having that hot Argentinian boy, who really didn't know I was alive, suddenly appear out of nowhere and offer to help while I scrubbed the word *JUEVOS* off my front door.

Wake up in the morning and declare what it is that you'll celebrate today. Even better, write it down. Celebrate all of it—the good, the bad, the not yet happened; the key is that you truly rejoice in the feeling of gratitude for *everything*.

There's a moment right before we give up or start rationalizing our way out of staying the course or begin to dip our toe into the sea of temptation that I like to call The Moment of Truth or Poof. It's the moment when all our no-nonsense dedication to achieving our goals and all our excitement about the brand-new life we're creating for ourselves either stays strong or goes poof into a La-Z-Boy–shaped puff of smoke. I strongly suggest having something at the ready to keep you on track when one of these moments flashes its sexy smile at you. Keep a note in your wallet that says something like, "This is your one and only life we're talking about here. Stay the course." Make a pact with a pal to be each other's emergency phone call when either one of you is dangling on the precipice of "screw it." Take a picture of the people or person who believes in you most giving you the thumbs up and stick it on the screen of your phone. Carry around a written statement of why you're so excited to change your life. Crank your favorite song, do a victory lap around your house, beat your chest and declare, "My ass is bad to the bone!" Have something specific and mighty meaningful in place to interrupt yourself should you begin negotiating your way out of going for your dreams. I mean it. Please do this, because a split second could mean the difference between completely changing your life or sliding back into ho-hummery.

You make a difference.

. . . .

make sure every single decision you make today is in alignment with your goal. "Is this sandwich I'm about to eat in alignment with my goal? Yes, I'm hungry, avocados are good for me and make me happy, this meal will give me energy. Sandwich, you officially have clearance."

"Is driving my kids to school in alignment with my goal? Yes, I will go home immediately afterward and start working, and having them the hell out of the house will be great for my focus."

"Is gossiping with Sheila at the coffee shop in alignment with my goal? No, it's a low-level activity in which Sheila and I try to heal our damaged self-esteems by ragging on others. Buh-bye, Sheila."

Keep your goal at the very forefront of your mind and be diligent about directing all your thoughts, focus, conversations, and actions in service of its success.

Write down any observations, victories, frustrations, and insights you may have from doing this today.

Ask your pals for support, your intuition for guidance, your boss for a day off, your neighbor to turn it down, your kids for a hug, your partner for an ear, your sister for help, the Universe for a miracle, the guy at the deli for a bigger pickle instead of the one he's about to give you—whatever it is, ask for what you want.

Notice where in your life you're feeling lacking and/ or let down by others and flex your asking muscle. This may sound like a no-brainer, but so often we shy away from reaching out and then we get resentful or depressed when people don't read our minds or the Universe doesn't provide.

Ask with specificity, clarity, and gratitude and ye shall receive.

Look around you right now and notice five things about your surroundings that bring you joy *that you've never paid much attention to before.* Things you appreciate regularly don't count—stretch yourself to notice how staggeringly abundant your Universe is by looking beyond what you usually see. For example, *All hail the light switch on the wall that provides me with the miracle of sight in the dark! Thank you neighborhood for making me feel safe and for having a nice, smiley mailman!* Notice five things, bask in all the reasons you love them, and then sit in a grateful stupor over what a charmed individual you are.

Your attitude steers the wheel
that determines the course of
your life.

. . . .

You are everything that brings you joy, lights you up, turns you on, holds your attention, fills your heart, cracks you up, makes you weep, calms you down, enlists your talents, inspires you to grow. . . .

It's all right there, inside yourself, everything you need to know about how to be the perfect expression of you. Trust your own gut, your own feelings, your own joy, above all else.

A few months ago, my brother took our aunt to the doctor and left with a diagnosis informing us all that she was in the beginning stages of Alzheimer's. As she's gotten older and has watched her memory slowly slipping away, the Big A has always been her biggest, most dreaded fear. So my brother, feeling devastated and scared for her as they were driving home from the doctor's, tearily let her know that we're all right here for her and that we will get through this together. "Get through what together?" she responded.

I'm not making light of a situation that breaks my heart, but I am rejoicing in the benefits of forgetfulness, something that tends to get a really bad rap in our culture. To her great credit, even Aunt Lucy, when she's lucid, is aware that her unawareness is a blessing because it frees her from worrying about something she has no control over.

Here are some other things we have no control over: the weather; the fact that we will die; other people's actions, reactions, opinions, beliefs, their love of puns, their inability to see how cute my dog is even when he's jumping all over them because he's so excited, which I know is annoying but his cuteness totally overshadows that. . . .

Change what you can change, accept what you cannot change, and every time you find yourself about to start stewing on something scary, irritating, or worrisome (practice staying aware of when this is happening, please), say to yourself, "I choose to forget this," and move on.

NOW = Never Over Whelmed

I would like to add to all the screaming and yelling about the importance of staying in the present moment by mentioning a benefit that's rarely discussed and here it is: *overwhelm* cannot touch you when you're all wrapped up in the here and now. Overwhelm is a mindset; it's the choice to focus on everything all at once and stress yourself out. Instead, choose to take your life moment by moment and savor it, like pulling bon-bons out of a heart-shaped box and popping them into your mouth, one by one.

Overwhelm exists in the future: "I have six trillion emails to answer, two kids to pick up at school, a blueberry pie to bake, four client calls, and a cat who just had kittens." Staying present while thoughtfully answering each email or while rolling out the pie crust or while getting a towel and cleaning up after the cats—each of these moments is its own deal, packed with so much to be grateful for and enjoy. These little moments have nothing to do with the mountain of madness they get lumped in with in the overwhelming future, so why make the choice to do that? Why not connect with and enjoy your moments on Earth like the great gifts they are?

I f you want to reach a new level of success in any area of your life, you *absolutely must* surround yourself with high-vibe people, or at least one high-vibe person whom you're in constant contact with.

Spend time with people who remind you—and who show you—that anything is possible. People who share their resources instead of their worries, who see your strengths, encourage your dreams, celebrate your successes, pooh-pooh your excuses, inspire you, stretch you, help you, and adore you.

Badassery doesn't happen in a vacuum. If you're serious about changing your life, get your power posse in place.

You can't take care of

anything or anyone if you

don't take care of yourself.

. . . .

next time you're in a waiting room somewhere or sitting on an airplane or stuck in bumper-to-bumper traffic, put away your cell phone and use the opportunity of forced downtime to strengthen your meditation practice. Here's a very basic and simple meditation you can get into and out of quickly and that you can do anywhere:

Close your eyes or stare at a spot on the floor in front of you with a loose gaze, part your lips a tiny bit to release your jaw, and focus all of your attention on the natural rhythm of your breath moving in and out of your body. Stay in that space, moving any thoughts that come into your mind to the side and coming back to your breath. Give this a try right now—set your alarm for five minutes and see how it goes. Get into the habit of making this your go-to activity when you're sitting around, instead of turning to your phone.

The more often you use your downtime to meditate and go inward and connect as opposed to distract yourself and go outward and get sucked into the virtual world, the more peaceful and happy you'll be.

Your intuition is your inner compass, it's a knowingness that transcends reason, it's a guide that gives nary a crap about anyone else's opinion, and it's the essence of who you are.

Your intuition is here to lead you through your purpose on Earth and to give you the answers you're seeking. What oh what could be more important than spending time getting good at connecting with something like *that*?

Here are some exercises to strengthen your relationship with your intuition that I would like you to do, please:

- Journal as free form and often as possible.
- Meditate every day.

- Pay close attention to the things and people and experiences that light you up, and involve yourself in those things.

- Listen to your words and get good at busting yourself when you're trying to talk yourself into something that doesn't fit, or out of something that does.

- Be on the lookout for intuitive "hits"—ideas that suddenly pop in, feelings about a person or a situation that just come to you, hunches, warnings, goose bumps, etc.—and practice following through on those instead of brushing them off.

Fear not the judgment of others; fear living a life in which you keep your wild, wonderful, weirdo self in a cage.

. . . .

When you next participate in the profound and wondrous miracle that is eating, chew your food for twice as long as you usually do. Focus on the contents in your mouth and explore all the tastes one by one, notice your saliva, behold how your tongue knows what to do. Then celebrate the food as it travels down to your stomach when you swallow and rejoice in all the nutrients it's supplying to support your dear, sweet, one and only body that's been your ride on your earthly journey from day one.

Send a big fat thank-you out to the Universe for your food, your body, your life.

Go about your day today as if this is your last day on Earth.

We humans think in images. For example, if I write the words *big bowl of pasta with marinara sauce and a glass of red wine*, an image of a big bowl of pasta with marinara sauce and a glass of red wine will pop into your head as you read them. And if you're like me, you're now seriously thinking of getting up and making a big bowl of pasta with marinara sauce and pouring a glass of red wine. My point? Images are incredibly powerful and motivating, they stir up strong feelings in us, they can even get the saliva flowing, and they act as a bridge for thoughts and ideas to be made manifest in physical form—we literally see our thoughts and words take physical form in our minds via imagery. How cool is that?

What I would like you to do today is utilize the power of imagery by finding a picture of your goal, achieved.

Flip through magazines or search online and print up an image that looks and feels exactly like the house you're wanting to build or the business you want to start or the experience you want to have and then look at it all day long. Feel the feelings this picture conjures, visualize yourself experiencing it as the truth, and keep this picture with you until the physical manifestation of it lands in your lap.

D on't take other people's negative energy personally. Other people's energy is just that: other people's energy. It's got nothing to do with you. If
your friend is pitching a fit because his frappé wasn't frap-
péed enough, whining and kvetching that this always
happens to him, it's his choice to perceive it as the
greatest injustice ever perpetrated against mankind and
to feel as if the entire world is against him. It's not
your job to tell him to calm down (which, you know,
always goes over real well when someone is losing it).
Let him have his experience while you focus on
other things like how interesting the artwork on
the walls of the café is or how blessed you are to have
lips to drink your coffee with or how delightfully frap-
péed your frappé is or how perhaps it's time to start

surrounding yourself with people who aren't such drama queens.

When someone lobs a temper tantrum in your direction, drop your catcher's mitt, leave the field, and let them pick it up themselves.

When you look in the mirror, the entire Universe is staring back at you. (Not to creep you out or anything.)

. . . .

The following is the most direct route to changing your life that I have to offer:

Visualize whatever new situation you are excited and totally not screwing around about creating for yourself. See it, feel it, own it, be it, shout it from the mountaintop, keep this energy strong.

Then . . .

Do something that will advance you toward this new reality that scares the holy heck out of you or that makes you extremely uncomfortable or that pushes you beyond what you once pretended your limits were. Repeat this drill every single day and your life will change so quickly you won't know what hit you. Bada bing. Bada boom.

I am a _____ magnet.

Fill in the blank with your noun of choice (money, man, woman, happiness, client, brilliant idea, free French fries, etc.). Say it all day long. Feel it. Believe it. Own it. Be it.

We *all* have the capacity to be brilliant, boring, sweet, mean, lazy, inspiring, stupid, generous, cheap, rich, poor, adorable, obnoxious, successful, pathetic, badass, lame-ass. The more you make a habit out of looking for the awesome, forgiving the fugly, and remembering that everyone is as lovable as they are flawed (including your sweet, stunning self), the happier you will be.

As we all know, the best course of action to take when your internet's not working or your computer's acting weird or your kid's rubbing peas on the wall is to unplug, turn it off, take a time-out.

Yet when we're trying, and failing, to get funding for our new business or the guy we just started dating isn't calling us back or we're writing page after page of profoundly sucky material and we've got a big presentation looming in the not-so-distant future, we tend to push harder, overanalyze, get self-critical. Meanwhile, success comes from being in the flow, not forcing it until something breaks.

Someone wise once said that you should meditate for an hour a day, unless you're really busy, then you should meditate for two.

If you're feeling stuck or frustrated, go for a stroll, take a nap, shop online for shoes, stare at the sky and play with your lip. It's not about giving up, it's about recharging, reconnecting, and remembering that we live in a Universe riddled with miracles.

Surrender attracts, desperation repels.

S it in a quiet place and close your eyes. Take a deep, expansive breath all the way into the very bottom of your stomach, hold it for three seconds and let it out slowly, intentionally, fully. Clear your mind of all thoughts and connect with the cells that make up your skin, your lungs, your mouth, your whole body, feel the energy moving through you from your thoughts, your feelings, your beliefs. Notice the vibrations of everything that makes up your mind, body, and soul comingling and interacting and buzzing about inside of you. Focus on the atoms that make up your clothes, the air around you, the floor you're sitting on, the trees outside, the water in the clouds above your head, the sun and the moon, the stars in the galaxy, and all the space in our infinite Universe. Sit for a moment and feel the energy within you, running through you, expanding out to all the Universe.

Imagine shifting a single atom of thought or feeling or physicality within you and visualize it rearranging all the energy within you and all the energy in the Universe.

Now visualize all the details of your desired reality, embody it with all your senses and all your feelings and feel the energy inside of you shifting and aligning itself with the vibration of this desired vision. Feel the movement of all the energy inside of you, and feel this new arrangement within you now expanding and rearranging and impressing your vision in energetic form on the cosmic force field of the Universe. Just like a single water droplet falling into the ocean affects, and is part of, the giant mass of water, every tiny energy shift within you affects, and is part of, the infinite cosmic field. Sit in this thrilling energetic space of your desired reality, hold it with you, revisit it as often as possible, and know that as you and the Universe come into energetic alignment with the vision of your new life, the vision is also taking shape in physical form on Earth.

If you keep waiting for the

right time,

you'll keep living the wrong

life.

. . . .

When I was a kid I had a stuffed animal that I named Scruffy after our neighbor's little white dog, a West Highland terrier, because he looked just like him. Scruffy was not the most high-end stuffed animal in my extensive collection. In fact, he was most likely the lowest on the low end. He had wiry white fur, was stuffed with hay, and was as flat as roadkill. Someone probably won him at a carnival by throwing a Ping-Pong ball at a goldfish in a cup or something. Regardless, he was one of my favorites and I brought him everywhere, which meant that on top of his already challenged physique, he was also filthy, matted, missing an eye, and had a hole in his stomach where the hay came out. My mother didn't try to hide her disgust, and on several occasions suggested he'd make a better flyswatter than bedmate, which she thought was all sorts of hilarious but she never got a laugh from me.

One day, while waiting nine hundred hours for my mother to finish talking to her friends in a supermarket parking lot, I investigated every inch of Scruffy out of boredom. His dirty little pink nose, his remaining green plastic eye, his long tail, his pointy little ears . . . and all of a sudden I realized something I'd never even considered before—Scruffy wasn't a dog, he was a cat! I know this doesn't sound like a big deal but I can still feel the shock and the terror. It was like having your dad slowly peel off his face to reveal he's actually the school principal and has been all along.

I had never questioned Scruffy's dogness because there was a dog who looked just like him in my immediate environment, which meant that's what dogs looked like, so Scruffy must be a dog. I didn't investigate, I just took what appeared before me as the truth. This is what happens to most of us when we grow up and start piecing together our perceptions of our worlds and ourselves—we take a quick look at the "reality" around us and figure, alrighty, this is how it is—noted! We go through life accepting these "truths," many of which make us miserable, and it isn't until we wake up and investigate that we suddenly discover unexpected and liberating insights hiding beneath our old dirty, scratchy beliefs.

Choose something that relates to your goal that you're currently struggling with or that has always tripped you up. A great way to get clear on what's going on with you is to really listen to how you talk and what you say about your quest. For example, let's say your goal is to meet your special someone. Listen to how you talk about dating or the availability of awesome single people or your skills as a flirter or your opinions of couples in general. Chances are excellent that if you're having trouble finding someone, your language and your beliefs about finding love aren't in alignment with what you say you desire.

Spend today talking and thinking and journaling about your goal and write down any negative thoughts or beliefs that come up for you and then investigate the crap out of them. For example, let's say you bust yourself on the thought that "if I meet someone he'll eventually cheat on me." You could then investigate that by asking, "Where did this belief come from? Are there any men out there who don't cheat? Is it possible that my awesome non-cheating guy exists and I just haven't met him yet?" Keep investigating your thought until it turns around— we are at the helm of how we perceive *everything,* so a turnaround is absolutely available if you keep peeling back the layers of your "reality." Once you unearth the rickety foundation of the truth you've been settling for, come up with a new belief or saying to replace the old one with, such as, "I'm in a happy and committed relationship with my loyal and loving man and I'm so excited I can barely stop squirming," and say it over and over until he walks into your life.

Really truly do this exercise, please. It sounds so simple but it can unlock the door to untold awesomeness.

otice five things that you love about yourself *that you've never focused on before*. The things you normally appreciate don't count—the point is to stretch yourself to notice how special you are by looking beyond what you usually see. For example, along with being great at your job, having a stellar sense of humor, being a loyal friend, an awesome parent, etc., perhaps you're extremely punctual *and* you have an excellent ear for harmony. Stretch yourself to notice how much wonderfulness you have to share with the world. Sit in a grateful stupor about what a lovable individual you are.

How would you behave if
the person you respected
most in the entire world
were watching?

. . . .

recently went to a brewery where they let people anonymously buy beers for other people who aren't there. So if you want to make your pal's day, you can buy her a beer, stick her name on the board, and then the next time she walks in she's like oh, wow, look at that, a free beer just for me!

I mean, how great is that?! What says I love you better than a free, anonymous beer?

My friend told me that she buys people beers all the time. In fact, she's got a business a few doors down and whenever she has to deal with a super-crotchety or annoying customer, she walks over to the brewery and buys them a free beer to clear the energy and let the conflict go.

I mean, how great is that?! What clears the energy and allows you to let go better than a free, anonymous beer?

I am so in love with all of this that I want you to think about ways you can do something special for the people around you too. Yes, even the people who annoy the crap out of you. Especially the people who annoy the crap out of you. Whether it's taking a moment to send them some love or finding compassion for them or getting them a little gift or making a point to really listen to them, make the conscious effort to give back in as many ways as you can today and notice how it shifts your energy.

Your job is to connect to your heart; get clear on what you desire; and align your thoughts, feelings, energy, and actions with this desire. That is your job.

The Universe will decide the how, the when, the where, and the what.

That is the Universe's job.

Have patience, faith, and gratitude, friend; patience, faith, and gratitude. It's all on the way.

You are closer than you think.

. . . .

ACKNOWLEDGMENTS

Enormous thanks to all the badasses out there who continue to show up, do the work, face their fears, and change the world by changing themselves. Equally gigantic thanks to my agent of awesomeness, Alexandra Machinist, for her smarts and support; my brilliant editor, Laura Tisdel, for her talent and nursing skills; and Jane Cavolina, Susan Johnson, Meredith Clark, Gabriel Levinson, and everyone else at Viking and Penguin Random House who worked their heinies off to get this book out at warp speed.

USER'S GUIDE